FVL

this man-
JESUS

this man-
JESUS

Written and Illustrated
by

DAVID MELTON

McGRAW-HILL BOOK COMPANY

New York   St. Louis   San Francisco   Montreal   Panama   Toronto

Acknowledgments

Many people contributed to this work. The author deeply appreciates the efforts, the joyous attitudes, and the influence these people so generously gave:

Nancy Melton, Kit Taylor, Deni Echterling, Mark Handler, Craig Bluin, Larry Feinberg, Russ Hall, Donald Klutz, Linda Jackson, Roddy Ely, Marsha Bingert, Rod Klutz, Traci Melton, Mary Jane Fulton, Lynda Schoeb, Barbara and Ronald Noel, Rosemarie and Homayoon Pasdar, Sue Ann Klutz, Rev. Robert E. Shaw, Marguerite Melton, Mary Etta Pearson, Ruby Thatch, Buz McKellips, Bob Askrin, and The White Masque Players—and a sincere appreciation to The Gospels of Matthew, Mark, Luke, and John.

Two thousand years ago, a man named Jesus walked the sandy stretches of a small, remote area of a land then known as Palestine. This man, Jesus, healed the sick and told the people how God expected them to live.

Although his ministry lasted for less than three short years, his teachings and his courage were destined to change the course of the world.

Jesus proclaimed himself to be the Son of Mankind and the Son of God. As the words he spoke became sacred, his raw courage and determination became examples for men to follow.

Because he talked of love and forgiveness, Jesus has often been depicted as a gentle and passive man. Although he possessed these qualities, it is obvious that he was also a bold and energetic rebel who challenged traditions and spoke out with such force that his own life was placed in danger.

During his lifetime, the name of Jesus and his teachings were heard only in that distant land. Since that time, the philosophies and the name of Jesus have been made known through-out the world.

Because I was unable to find a book which depicted Jesus with the energy and the force that I wanted to present to my children, I entered into the preparation of this book.

I dedicate this book to my children, Todd and Traci, to my sister's children, Amy and Kim, and to all the children who will share the images and the teachings of this man, Jesus.

David Melton

Isaiah, the Prophet,
told the people of Israel
that God would send
his Son to Earth
to live as a man
and to walk among men.

"When it is time,
you will know,"
Isaiah said,
"for there will come

a man from the wilderness
who will tell you."

Some people thought
the Son of God
would come as a king
to rule over the land.
But others believed
he would come
as a common man
from a simple home.

ISAIAH (The Prophet)—In the history of the Jewish people, there were men who believed themselves to be the spokesmen of God. They spent much of their time commenting on the morals and the religious attitudes of the people and revealing the thoughts of God to them. Although it was not the prophets' basic role, they sometimes would predict things that were to occur in the future. Living about 700 years before Jesus was born, Isaiah is considered to have been one of the four great prophets in Biblical history. He stressed to the people that they should have complete faith in God's power and believe that he would protect those who trusted Him.

ISRAEL—was originally another name for Jacob. It was commonly used to designate the descendants of Jacob's twelve sons (as the children of Israel), and was later applied to the people of Judah. These people, at different times in history, are referred to as the Hebrews, the Israelites, and the Jews.

Hundreds of years later,
out of the wilderness,
there came such a man.
He was called
John, the Baptist.

This man, John,
walked along the banks
of the Jordan River,
telling the people
that soon
they would see
the Son of God.

Crowds of people came
from Jerusalem,
from the Jordan Valley,
and all parts of Judea
to see this man, John —
this man from the wilderness —
this man who wore clothes
made of camel's hair —

this man who ate
locust beans
and wild honey —
this man, John,
John, the Baptist.

Many of the people
who gathered to see him,
listened to his words
and became ashamed
for wrongs they had done.
And John baptized them
in the Jordan River.

Some of these people
began to wonder
if this man, John,
was the Son of God —
the Christ
who had been promised.
But John told them
that he was not the one.

JOHN, THE BAPTIST — was born in the hill country of Judea. He and Jesus were cousins. They were about the same age, however, John was probably born six months earlier. He was about twenty-eight years of age when he began preaching. He preached about the coming of the Son of God and gathered many followers. It is thought that some of his followers later became disciples of Jesus. John was later arrested at the command of Herod Antipas. It is not certain how long he was in prison before he was executed.

BAPTISM — is the act of dipping a person into water or sprinkling water on him. It symbolizes the washing away of past sins and the introduction of the person into a new way of life.

From the simple home
of a carpenter
there came a man—
a man who would
later be called,
The Man from Nazareth,
The Promised One,
The King of the Jews,
The Son of Mankind,
and The Son of God.

This was the man
Isaiah told about.
This was the man
John had promised.
This was the man—
this man, Jesus.

And Jesus came
to the Jordan River
and walked into the water
to be baptized by John.
When Jesus came up
out of the water,
the Spirit of God appeared
in the form of a dove.
And a voice
was heard, saying,
"This is my beloved Son
in whom I am well pleased."

And the Spirit of God
led Jesus away
and took him
into the desert.

PALESTINE—is one of the most famous lands in the world. Lying between Egypt and Syria, it is bordered on the east by the Arabian Desert, and on the west by the Mediterranean Sea. Almost 2000 years before Jesus was born, Abraham led the Hebrew people into this area, then called Canaan, the promised land. The Hebrew people were the first to believe in one God. During the 2000 years that passed between Abraham and the birth of Jesus, armies of five nations (Assyria, Babylon, Persia, Greece and Rome), conquered Palestine and ruled the land and the people. At the time Jesus was born, Palestine was ruled by the Roman Empire. The Romans ruled harshly and oppressed the people of Israel. The Jewish people were hoping for a miracle or, at least, a leader who would drive the armies of Rome out of their land. So it was a time of great conflict and political maneuvers.

GALILEE—was the northernmost region of Palestine where Jesus spent much of his life.

NAZARETH—was a small town in Galilee; the home of Joseph, Mary and Jesus.

While Jesus stayed
alone in the desert
forty days and forty nights,
he had nothing to eat.

And the Spirit of Satan
came to him and said,
"If you are really
the Son of God,
then turn these rocks
into loaves of bread."
Jesus answered,
"Man does not live
on food alone;
he also needs
the truth of God."

Satan decided to try again.
Standing on the top
of the tallest temple,
Satan said to Jesus,
"If you are really
the Son of God,
jump from this high place.
His angels will protect you
and you will not be hurt."

And Jesus answered,
"Man should not test God
or his angels."

Satan decided to try
once more to tempt Jesus.
On the highest mountain,
Satan showed him visions
of the richest cities
and said to him,
"I will give you
all these cities
and all their riches
if you will worship me
instead of God."
And Jesus answered,
"Take these visions away
and leave me alone.
I will worship God
and no other."

Seeing that he
could not tempt Jesus
with riches and power,
Satan backed away
and left him alone.

SATAN—was considered to be the power of evil; the opposite of good; and the enemy of God. He is called by many names—Satan, Beelzebub, The Devil, and The Evil One.

And when Jesus came
out of the desert,
he walked to
the Sea of Galilee.
There, he saw
two fishermen,
who were brothers,
casting their nets
into the waters.
Jesus called them by name,
Peter and Andrew,
and said to them,
"Follow me,
and I will make you
fishers of men."
The two brothers
left their nets
and followed Jesus.

When they had gone
a short distance,
Jesus called the names
of two other fishermen,
James and John,

and they too,
became his followers.
Later, Jesus called
eight other men
to follow him.
They were: Andrew, Philip,
Thaddaeus, Thomas, James,
Bartholomew, and Simon.
The twelfth man
was named Judas Iscariot.

As they followed Jesus
along the country roads
and into the cities,
they saw the wonders
that this man could do.

This man, Jesus,
could reach out
and touch those
who were sick
or crippled
or blind
and make them well.

PETER (Simon called Peter)—was a master fisherman on the Lake of Galilee. He became one of Jesus' closest friends and one of his most faithful followers. He was enthusiastic and eager, but quick in making mistakes. It is thought that he may have been a follower of John, the Baptist, before he met Jesus. After Jesus was crucified, Peter assumed leadership of the disciples and was the first to perform a miracle in the name of Jesus by healing a cripple. Peter became renowned as a healer and preacher. Little is known about his work outside of Palestine; however, it appears that he traveled to Antioch and may have visited Corinth. It is said that he went to Rome during the reign of Nero and was crucified there. Insisting that he was unworthy to be killed in the same way as Jesus, he asked to be nailed on the cross upside down.

Soon,
all the people of Galilee
heard about this healer,
and this teacher—
this man,
this man, Jesus.
And they came
in large crowds
to see him
and hear his words.

One morning
when Jesus met
a large crowd
that waited for him,
he led the people
to a hillside.

Jesus said to them:
"There are blessings
which God gives
to humble people—
He offers them
a place in Heaven.
And God has blessings

for those who are sad
and worried—
they will be comforted.
The gentle and willing people
are also blessed—
someday, my world
will belong to them.
Blessed are those
who treat others fairly—
they will be fairly treated.
Blessed are the kind people
who give mercy to others—
they shall receive mercy.
Blessed are
the pure in heart—
for they shall see God.
Blessed are those
who work for peace—
for they are truly
the children of God.
Blessed are the people
who pray to God
and believe his words.
Because of their beliefs,
they will be remembered."

ANDREW—was a fisherman and a brother of Simon Peter. It is thought that he may have been a follower of John, the Baptist, before he became one of the first of Jesus' twelve disciples. It is believed that after Jesus was crucified, Andrew traveled as far as Scythia (which is now the southern slopes of Russia and the Ukraine), preaching and healing the sick. It is said that he was persecuted because of his teachings, imprisoned, and at about sixty years of age, he was crucified on an X-shaped cross.

And Jesus said:
"If men sometimes
tell lies about you
and laugh at you,
and if you suffer pain
because you follow
my teachings—
be brave
and be happy,
for you are not alone.
Others have lived
and others have died
for their beliefs.
Your reward
will be not on Earth.
It will be in Heaven.

You are the future
of the world.
You must stand up
for what you believe
and not keep it secret.
Go and tell others
all the things
that I teach you."

And when they asked
if he had come
to change the laws
Moses had given them
many years before,
Jesus answered
that he had not.
He had come
to give the laws
more meaning
and fuller understanding.

"You are to honor
the laws of Moses
and do even more,"
Jesus told them.
"If you break these laws
or teach others
to break them,
you shall be less
in the sight of God.
But if you obey the laws
and teach others to honor them,
then your reward
shall be great.

LAWS OF MOSES (or Mosaic Law)—The religion of the Old Testament was based upon instructions from God, believed to have been given to Moses on Mount Sinai. The Ten Commandments are the heart of these laws.

The laws say
that if you kill,
then you must be killed,"
Jesus said.
"I add to that rule
and tell you that even
if you become angry
at other people,
then you will be judged
for your anger.

If you are making
an offering to God
and suddenly remember
that you have been
unkind to another person,
leave your offering
and go to that person
and tell him
that you are sorry.

There is an old saying—
'Love your friends
and hate your enemies.'
But I say to you,

Love your enemies also,
and pray for them.
In this way,
you will be acting
as the children of God.

If you love
only those who love you,
how are you different?
Even evil men can do that.
If you are friendly
only to those
who are friendly to you,
then how are you different?
Even the wicked do that.

You are to behave
in such ways
that other people can
learn by your actions.
As God is generous,
you, too, should be giving.
As God is perfect,
then you, too, should
strive for perfection."

JAMES—was one of the first disciples of Jesus. He was a brother of John. They were fishermen and may have been partners of Simon Peter and Andrew. These four men were believed to have been the closest to Jesus. After the crucifixion of Jesus, James, along with John, Peter and Andrew, energetically worked in preaching and healing. It is said that James traveled in northwest Spain. Fifteen years after he left his fishing nets to become a disciple, he was killed by Herod Agrippa. In Acts 12:1-3, James' death is described: "He killed James, the brother of John, with a sword." This is considered to be the only reliable Biblical record of the death of any of the disciples, and it is believed that James was the first disciple to die.

And Jesus warned:
"Take care.
Don't do good deeds
just for attention.
Instead,
do them in secret.
You know what you do,
therefore God knows.
That's what is important.

And when you pray,
don't say your prayers
just to show other people
that you are praying.
Instead,
go away by yourself,
all alone,
and close the door
and pray in secret.
God knows your secrets,
and it is to God
you should be praying."

The people asked,
"How should we pray?"

And Jesus answered,
"Pray in this way:
Our Father—in Heaven,
we honor your name.
Your kingdom will come,
your plans will be done,
here on Earth
as they are
in Heaven.
Give us today
the things we need.
Forgive us
for the wrongs
we do to others,
as we forgive those
who do wrong to us.
Please don't place
temptations before us,
and keep us from evil.
For we know
yours is the kingdom,
and the power
and the glory,
Forever,
Amen."

JOHN—(a son of Zebedee), was a Galilean fisherman and a brother of James—probably from the town of Bethsaida. John may have been a follower of John, the Baptist, before he became a disciple of Jesus. It appears that the Zebedee family was of some substance and influence. John and James were given the nicknames of the "Boanerges" (sons of Thunder), perhaps because they had fiery tempers. It is thought by many that he was the author of the Gospel of John, although others feel that it was written by another man with the same name.

And Jesus
told the people,
"If you forgive
those who
do wrong to you,
then you will be forgiven.
But if you don't
forgive others,
then God will not
forgive the wrongs
which you do.

Don't worry about
material things
because you are here
for only a short time.
Don't place your thoughts
on money and possessions,

for these things
can be lost or stolen.
Place your thoughts
on those things
that keep you close to God,
for they cannot
be lost or taken away.

If you have
only good thoughts
in your mind,
there will be sunshine
in your soul.
But if you
allow your thoughts
to become dark and evil,
then your soul will
become clouded with darkness.

MATTHEW—was a tax collector from Capernaum who became one of Jesus' twelve disciples. There is very little known about Matthew. By tradition, it is considered that he was the author of the first Gospel, however, many Biblical scholars maintain that the Gospel of Matthew is carefully compiled from three sources—the Gospel of Mark and two collections of sayings of Jesus, which may have been written by Matthew. There are various legends about Matthew's death. Conflicting stories say he died in Ethiopia, in Persia, and in Ponteus on the Black Sea.

Don't worry about
food and clothing,"
Jesus said.
"For you already have
a life and a body—
they are far more important
than what you eat or wear.

Look at the birds.
They don't worry
about tomorrow's food.
They don't build storehouses.
God's Earth feeds them.
God cares more for you
than he does for birds.

And don't worry
about your fine clothes.
Look at the flowers
in the fields—
they don't worry
about how they are dressed.

Still they are beautiful.
And if God cares
so well for flowers
which are here
for only today
and gone tomorrow,
then, surely,
he cares much more
for you.

Have you so little faith
that you can't see this?

Take care of each day
a day at a time.
Don't waste today
worrying about tomorrow.
Live and make the most
of each day and every day.
If God will help you today,
he will also
help you tomorrow."

PHILIP—There is little doubt that he was a follower of John, the Baptist, before becoming a disciple of Jesus because it is written that Jesus called to him from the banks of the Jordan River where John was baptizing. Philip was probably a fisherman from Bethsaida, the same town on the Lake of Galilee where Peter and Andrew lived. After Jesus was crucified, it is said that Philip traveled to Samaria, Gaza and Caesarea, preaching and performing miracles, and that he became a bishop in Lydia. Traditions contradict each other—one says Philip died in Hieroplis and another says that he was also crucified.

The people listened
to the things Jesus said.

"If a child asks his father
for a loaf of bread,
would his father
give him a stone instead?
Of course not.
Fathers give their children
the things they need.
Since God is the Father
of all living things,
he will provide gifts
for those who ask him.

Treat all other people
as you want them
to treat you.

All who listen
to my instructions
and follow them
are as wise as the man
who builds his house
on solid rock.
When the rains come,

and the waters rise,
and the storms beat
against his house,
it does not crumble,
for it stands on rock.
But those who listen
to my instructions
and do not follow them,
are as foolish
as the man who
builds his house on sand.
For when the rains come,
and the waters rise,
and the storms beat
against his house,
it will fall
with a mighty crash."

This man, Jesus,
was not like the teachers
who taught in the temples.
He spoke simply and
directly to the people.
This man, Jesus,
was like no other man
they had ever seen.

THOMAS—was the loyal and practical disciple of Jesus. After Jesus came back from death, Thomas refused to believe it unless he "saw" the prints of the nails in his hands and...placed his hand in Jesus' side (John 20:25). Jesus allowed him to do so. Legend says that Thomas traveled to Persia and Southern India, and began a church there. Some say he was violently killed, but it is not certain.

As Jesus traveled with
his twelve followers,
they often laughed,
and had good times together.
People who saw them
realized that these
were happy men.

When they came to a village,
they were welcome
because this man, Jesus,
and his followers
loved to be with people.
And people liked
to be with them.

Jesus often told stories,
and the people

enjoyed hearing them.

Once, his followers
scolded the mothers
for bringing their children
and started to send them away.
But when Jesus saw this,
he called out,
"Don't take the children away.
Let them come closer to me,
for all of God's gifts
belong to them."
Jesus took the little children
into his arms
and loved them.
And placing his hands
upon their heads,
he blessed them.

SEA OF GALILEE—is the largest fresh water lake in Palestine. It is nearly thirteen miles long and eight miles wide and is fed, primarily, by the Jordan River.

One day,
Jesus called together
his twelve followers,
and said to them,
"If you are
truly my men,
you must leave
all other things behind you.
You must love me more
than you love
even your own families.
One day soon,
it will be your job
to tell all people
that the love of God
is close to them.
You will heal the sick
and teach others
what I have taught you.
Don't take money
for what you do,
and don't take
extra clothing with you.
You will not need
these earthly things,
for those you help

will, in return,
feed you and care for you.
The things that I tell you
in the shadows
you will say openly
in the light of day.
The things that
I whisper in your ears
you will shout
from the rooftops.

I send you as sheep
to walk among wolves.
You must be careful—
there will be those
who will arrest you
and will hurt you.
But don't be afraid.
They can hurt your bodies,
but they can't touch your souls.

Those who welcome you
will be welcoming me.
And when they welcome me,
they are also welcoming God,
for it is God who sent me."

THADDAEUS—(sometimes referred to as Lebbaeus), was one of the twelve disciples. There is very little written about Thaddaeus. Some believe he was also referred to as Judas, a son of James (or that he was James' brother). It is not known what happened to him.

Because John, the Baptist,
had said, openly,
that King Herod was
a wicked and sinful man,
the King had John arrested
and locked in prison.
After some time,
John, the Baptist,
was beheaded.

When Jesus heard
that John had been killed,
he went out
by himself
to be alone.
But the crowds saw him,
and they followed him.

In the evening,
his followers came to him
and said,
"It is past time for supper,
and there is nothing to eat.
Shall we send the crowds away?"
But Jesus replied,
"That's not necessary.

You will feed them."
"What?" they exclaimed.
"There is not enough food.
We have only
five loaves of bread
and two fish!"
"Bring them to me,"
Jesus told them.
And when they brought
the five loaves of bread
and the two fish,
Jesus looked toward the sky
and asked God
to bless the food.
Then Jesus broke apart
the loaves of bread.
Baskets of bread and fish
were carried into the crowd
of five-thousand people,
and everyone ate
until they were full.

And when everyone had eaten,
there were twelve baskets
of bread and fish
left over.

KING HEROD ANTIPAS—was a son of Herod the Great. It is said that Herod Antipas was an idle, vicious and extravagant King who built the castle and town of Tiberias on the northeast coast of the Sea of Galilee. Although he is referred to as "king" in the Bible, it is questioned that he ever held the title. He requested the title from the Roman Emperor but there is no record showing that it was given to him. His title was probably Tetrarch of Galilee. According to the Gospels, Herod divorced his wife to marry Herodias. At Herod's birthday party, Herodias' daughter, Salome, danced and Herod was so pleased that he said he would give her whatever she desired. Salome went to her mother and said, "What shall I ask for?" And her mother told her to ask for the head of John, the Baptist. Although Herod Antipas didn't want John killed, he kept his word to Salome. He sent a soldier to the prison to behead John and had the head of the Baptist brought on a platter and placed before the young woman. Herod Antipas was killed when his armies were defeated by the soldiers of King Aretas of Arabia about three years after Jesus was crucified.

After supper,
Jesus told his followers
to sail their boat
to the other side of the lake.
When they had gone,
Jesus went into the hills
and there, he prayed.

Evening fell into darkness
and out on the lake
a terrible storm began to blow.
When waves lashed higher
than the boat,
his followers became afraid
and cried out for help.
Suddenly, they looked out
across the raging waters and
saw Jesus walking toward them.
They screamed in terror
for they thought he was a ghost.
But the voice of Jesus said,
"Don't be afraid."
Peter called back,
"Is it really you?"
"It is I," Jesus replied.
And he told Peter

to walk toward him.
So Peter climbed from the boat
and walked across the water
toward Jesus.
But when Peter stopped
to look at the waves
that surrounded him,
he became frightened again
and began to sink.
"Save me, Lord!" he cried out.
Jesus reached out
and touched Peter's hand,
and he stood on the water again.
Then the followers watched
as Jesus commanded the winds
and the waters to be still.
As he ordered,
the sea and the sky
became quiet and calm.
Then Jesus asked his followers,
"Why were you so frightened?
Do you have so little faith?"
His followers sat down
and thought about the wonders
they had seen
of this man, Jesus.

BARTHOLOMEW—was one of the twelve disciples. Bartholomew means, literally, son of Tolmai. Most Bible scholars agree that his real name was Nathaniel. It is believed that he was born in the small village of Cana, in Galilee, and was introduced to Jesus by Philip. After Jesus was crucified, it is said that Bartholomew traveled as far as India telling of Jesus, and that he met a violent death by being skinned alive in Armenia.

Before Jesus entered
the city of Jerusalem,
he sent two followers ahead.
"As you enter the city,"
he told them,
"you will see a donkey.
Bring it to me.
If anyone asks
what you are doing,
just tell them,
'Our Master needs it,
but it will be returned soon.'"
The two followers
brought the donkey
and laid their coats
across its back
for Jesus to sit upon.

As Jesus entered the city,
large crowds of people
lined the streets of Jerusalem.
When they saw Jesus,
many ran into the streets
and spread their coats
and leafy branches
upon the ground before him.
The people honored Jesus
in the same way
they would be expected
to honor a king.
As he rode through the city,
the crowds followed him.
They called out,
"Praise him!"
Praise him!"

JAMES—(a son of Alphaeus) was also one of Jesus' twelve disciples. It is thought by some that James and Thaddaeus were related to each other in some way. There is not sufficient evidence to identify him as either James, the brother of Jesus, or James, the Younger.

When Jesus entered the Temple,
he saw money lenders inside
and merchants selling goods.
Seeing the house of God
being so misused,
Jesus became extremely angry.
He turned over the tables,
tore down the stalls,
and drove the money lenders
from the building.
"The Temple of God
is a place of prayer!"
he scolded them.
"But you have turned it
into a den of robbers!"

The Chief Priests
and Jewish Leaders demanded,
"Who gave you the right
to send these people out?"
Jesus replied,
"I will answer your question
if you will answer mine."
Then Jesus asked them,
"Was John the Baptist
sent here by God?"

The question worried the Priests
because so many people
would hear their answer.
They talked among themselves.
"If we answer, 'Yes,'
then this Jesus will say,
'Why did you allow
John to be killed?'
But if we say, 'No,
John was not sent by God,'
then the people might
run us out of the Temple."
So they turned to Jesus
and said, "We do not know.
Therefore, we cannot answer."
"Then I will not answer
your question either,"
Jesus replied.

After Jesus and his followers
left the Temple,
the Chief Priests
and the Jewish Leaders
began to plan ways
to get this man, Jesus,
out of their way.

JERUSALEM—was the capital city of Israel, known as the Holy City. It was the city of David, center of his monarchy. King Solomon's greatest contribution to the city was the building of the Temple. Jesus preached in the city, was arrested, tried, and crucified there. The city of Jerusalem was destroyed by the Romans seventy years after Jesus' death.

During the days
of the Passover,
the Chief Priests
and the Jewish Leaders
decided to arrest Jesus
and have him killed.
Although Jesus realized
his life was in danger,
he sent two of his followers
back into Jerusalem.
"You will see a man
with a jug of water,"
Jesus told them.
"He will show you to a room.
Prepare our supper there."

In the evening hours,
Jesus and his followers
came to the room
and ate their supper.
When they had finished,
Jesus took a bowl of water,
and bending down
as a servant might,
he began to wash
the feet of his friends.

But Peter pulled away, saying,
"I will not allow you
to wash my feet.
I should wash yours, Lord."
Jesus replied,
"If you won't allow it,
you cannot be my follower."
Hearing this, Peter exclaimed,
"Then wash not only my feet,
but wash my hands
and my head as well,
for I am with you."

After he had finished,
Jesus asked his followers,
"Do you understand
what I have done?
You call me Master and Lord,
which is right for you to say
because it is true.
But since I am the Lord
and the Teacher,
I am also your servant.
You too should be
as servants to each other—
and to all people as well."

PASSOVER—is the Hebrew festival, celebrated in spring, which commemorates God's deliverance of his people from slavery in Egypt and, particularly, the "passing over" of the Hebrew homes when the Egyptian children were slain.

Then Jesus said,
"But I do not say
these things to all of you.
For there is one
in this room
who will betray me."
The followers
looked at one another
wondering who
would do such a thing.
Then Jesus handed
a piece of bread
to Judas Iscariot
and told him,
"Now, go quickly,
and do what you will."

Judas understood,
but the others did not.
Some thought since
Judas carried the money,
that Jesus was telling
him to pay for the food
or to give money to the poor.
Judas left at once
and went out
into the night.

After Judas had gone,
Jesus said,
"My time has come.
I soon must leave you."
"Where are you going?"
Peter questioned.
Jesus answered,
"You can't go with me,
but you will follow."
"Why can't I go with you?"
Peter asked,
"for I am ready
to go to prison
and even to die for you."
And Jesus told him,
"Before the rooster crows
tomorrow morning, Peter,
three times, you will deny
that you ever knew me."
"No!" Peter cried out.
"Not even if I die,
I will never deny you!"
And the others
promised the same.

JUDAS ISCARIOT—Of all the twelve disciples, perhaps Judas Iscariot's name is most remembered. His act of betraying Jesus, certainly, has set him apart as one of the villains in history. His motives for the betrayal are not made clear in the Gospels, so Judas has become a much discussed character and many theories have been drawn for his actions. At first glance it might seem that Judas was greedy and acted for money, but since Jesus made him treasurer of the group, this is questionable. It is also thought that Judas was disappointed that Jesus did not announce himself as the Messiah while in Jerusalem and gather the people to support his claim, and that his betrayal might force Jesus to perform a miracle to save himself. The death of Judas is referred to in two ways: 1) Matthew tells that in remorse, he hanged himself and 2) in Acts it is told that Judas died, accidentally.

And now, when Jesus
and his followers went
to The Garden of Gethsemane,
he told them,
"I am filled with sorrow.
Stay here with me and pray."

Then Jesus walked
a little further
and fell to his knees.
"Father," he prayed,
"if it is possible,
take this sorrow from me —
but I will do
what you want."

Jesus walked back
and found that
his followers were asleep.
Waking them, he asked,
"Couldn't you wait
for even one hour?
Now, watch and pray with me,
for although my spirit is strong,
my body is weak."

Jesus went away to pray again,
and when he returned
they were asleep.
Again, he awakened them,
and once more
he went back to pray.

When he came back
the third time,
and saw they were sleeping,
he said to them,
"Sleep on and rest."
But then he looked up
and saw the Chief Priests
and the Jewish Leaders,
with swords and clubs,
coming toward him.
And when he saw that
Judas Iscariot
was also with them,
Jesus told his followers,
"Come, wake up.
The time for sleep is ended.
Wake up! Wake up!
My betrayer is here."

CHIEF PRIESTS AND JEWISH LEADERS — were officials of two of the three main sects of Jews — the Phari-sees and Sadducees. Both parties would have viewed Jesus as a rebel and his teachings and popularity with the people as a threat to their traditions.

PHARISEES — were the most powerful religious and political group in Palestine when Jesus lived. The group was composed of businessmen, shopkeepers, teachers, and some priests. They criticized Jesus for healing the sick on the Sabbath and maintained that he, repeatedly, taught against the Laws of Moses. Jesus, on the other hand, denounced the Pharisees for their outward displays of religious traditions.

SADDUCEES — were a political-religious party of Jews consisting largely of priests and aristocrats. Their High Priests held a monopoly on the sale of animals for sacrifice. They did not believe in an after life except among the shades of Sheol (Hell). They were firm believers in the Law, and they did not accept the ideas of angels and spirits.

As the Chief Priests
and the Leaders waited,
Judas walked up to Jesus
and kissed him on the cheek,
which was the signal
to the crowd
that this man was Jesus.

As they arrested Jesus
and tied his hands,
one of his followers
pulled out a sword
and slashed off an ear
of one of the men.
"Put away the sword,"
Jesus ordered.
"Those who use swords
will be killed by swords."
Jesus reached out and
when he touched the man
his ear was healed.

Then Jesus turned
and asked the Priests,
"Am I so dangerous
that you had to bring
all these people
with swords and clubs
to take me?
I was often with you
teaching in the temple.
Why didn't you
arrest me then?"
The Priests and the Leaders
would not answer.
"I see," said Jesus.
"Then this is the way
it is meant to be."

By this time,
the followers of Jesus
had run away
and were hiding.

SIMON—was one of the twelve disciples. It is considered that he was a member of the Zealot party, a fanatic nationalist group whose guerrilla tactics were activated against the Roman rule. Little else is known about him with certainty. Some believe Simon was killed in Persia.

The mob led Jesus
to the house
of the High Priest.
There, the Jewish Leaders
were gathered to hear
false witnesses tell
lies about Jesus.
"We heard this man,"
one witness swore,
"say that he could
tear down God's Temple
and rebuild it
in three days."
The High Priest asked Jesus
if he had said these things.
Jesus did not answer.

Then the High Priest asked,
"Do you claim to be
the Son of God?"
And Jesus answered,
"Yes,
I am the Son of Mankind,

and in the future,
you will see
that I am
also the Son of God."

Hearing this,
the High Priest
cried out in anger
and tore at his own clothing.
"Lies!
Lies against God!"
And he turned to
the other Priests.
"We need no other witness.
You heard what he said.
He lies!
He claims to be the Son of God.
What shall we do with him?"
The other Priests
and the Jewish Leaders
cried out,
"Kill him!
Kill him!"

MARK—(or John Mark), was a young man in his early teens during the ministry of Jesus. He became a friend of Paul and later of Peter. It is believed that he wrote the Gospel from memories told to him by Peter. It is also considered by many Bible scholars that Mark wrote his Gospel first, and that Matthew and Luke wrote theirs later, and were influenced by his writings.

Meanwhile,
Peter was standing outside
in the courtyard.
A girl came to him
and she said,
"Didn't I see you
with this man, Jesus?"
"No," Peter answered,
and walked away.

Later, by the gate,
a woman saw him
and she said to the others,
"This is a follower of Jesus."
"No," Peter said firmly,
"No, I am not.
I don't even know this man,"
and he moved away.

After a while,
some men walked
over to him and said,
"We know that you
are one of his followers."
This time Peter
became angry
and he screamed out,
"No!
I am not one of his followers.
I do not know the man!"

Then in the distance,
Peter heard a rooster crow,
and he remembered
what Jesus had told him.
And he ran away
and cried.

LUKE—Although his name is mentioned only twice in the Bible, he is thought to be the author of the Third Gospel, and the Acts of the Apostles. He was a loyal secretary, physician, and companion of the Apostle Paul. He accompanied Paul from Troas in Asia Minor to Philippi in Greece. Six years later, they returned to Jerusalem together and then he went with Paul from Caesarea to Rome. It is thought that Luke died in Greece at the age of eighty-four; however, other stories say that he was killed because of his beliefs.

When morning came,
the Chief Priests
and the Jewish Leaders
bound Jesus in chains
and took him to Pontius Pilate,
the Roman Governor.
They hoped to persuade
the Romans to kill Jesus.

While the Priests
told lies about him,
Jesus remained silent.
Finally,
Pilate asked Jesus,
"Do you claim to be
the King of the Jews?"
"You say that I am,"
Jesus answered.
"And did you say that
you would destroy the temples?"
Pilate questioned.
But to Pilate's surprise,
Jesus said nothing.

It was the custom
that each year during
the Passover holidays,
the Roman Governor
would free one Jewish prisoner.
That year, there was
a well-known prisoner
named Barabbas.
As crowds gathered
outside Pilate's house,
the Priests and the Leaders
talked with them.
So, when Pilate asked them
which prisoner to free,
Barabbas or Jesus,
the crowd called back,
"Barabbas!"
"Then what shall I do
with this man, Jesus?"
Pilate asked.
And they shouted,
"Crucify him!
Crucify him!"

PONTIUS PILATE—was the fifth Roman Governor to rule over Judea, Samaria and Idumea. He was approximately the same age as Jesus—in his early thirties. He held his post of governor for about ten years. He was a proud, hot tempered man and was extremely unpopular with the people. While in Palestine, he made his home in Caesarea, a city by the Mediterranean Sea. However, during Jewish Holidays, especially the Passover, he traveled to Jerusalem to command his soldiers because rioting was more frequent at these times. It is obvious that the trial of Jesus was a political maneuver and that Pilate realized this. Although Pilate was convinced that Jesus was innocent of the charges brought against him by the Priests and Jewish Leaders, he was afraid that if he did not give in to the demands of these influential men, his army would be faced with massive riots. So he allowed Jesus to be crucified. Traditions and legends contradict each other as to what later became of Pilate. Some say he was executed by Nero. Some say he was banished to Vienne, and others say that he committed suicide. Whatever happened to him, there is little doubt that he ever forgot the day that Jesus of Nazareth stood before him.

And the crowd cheered
as Barabbas was set free.
Then Pilate ordered
his soldiers to take Jesus
and whip him.
After they had whipped him,
the soldiers dressed Jesus
in a purple robe.
They made a crown of thorns
and placed it upon his head.
They laughed at him.
They spit at him.
They bowed before him.
"Hail, King of the Jews!"
they mocked.

When Judas Iscariot
saw what was happening,
he was sorry
that he had betrayed Jesus.
He tried to return
the money the Chief Priests
had given him,
and he begged them
to free Jesus.
But they refused.

Judas threw the money
on the floor
and ran out of the Temple.
Crying in sorrow,
and in madness,
he went, alone,
into the fields,
and hanged himself.

Although Pilate could
find no wrong in Jesus,
he realized that
if he resisted
the will of the crowd,
they might riot.
He had a bowl of water
brought to him.
"I want all to see,"
Pilate told them,
"that I have no part
in the killing of this man.
It is your decision,
not mine.
I wash my hands.
I am not responsible
for what you now do."

BARABBAS — was the Jewish prisoner who was released in preference to Jesus. He was probably a Zealot, and a member of the Sicarii, a guerilla group that was called, literally, the "dagger men," who fought against the Roman occupation forces.

Then, Jesus was led
to a lonely place
called "The Skull,"
and there,
between two robbers,
he was crucified
upon a wooden cross.
A signboard was placed
above his head.
It read,
"Jesus,
King of the Jews."

There were people
who laughed
and jeered at him.
"Look at you now!"
they yelled,
"King of the Jews!
Let's see you
destroy the Temple now!"
And the Priests laughed
and called out to him,
"If you are truly
the Son of God,

then prove it
by saving yourself!"
Jesus did not answer.
Instead, he prayed aloud,
"Forgive them, God.
They do not realize
the evils they do."

About noon,
a darkness fell
across the land.
It lasted
for three hours.
Jesus called out,
"My God, my God,
Don't leave me!"
When he asked for water,
a sponge of vinegar
was held to his lips.
At last,
Jesus cried out,
"Father,
I give my spirit to you."
After saying these words,
Jesus died.

CRUCIFIXION—was a form of execution used by various ancient peoples. The condemned was fastened to a wooden cross, usually with ropes and sometimes nails, subjected to public shame, and left to die a lingering, painful death of fatigue, exposure, and starvation. It was considered the lowest and most humiliating of ways to be put to death.

In the evening hours,
Joseph of Arimathea,
a rich and powerful man,
asked Pilate for permission
to take the body of Jesus.
And Joseph went
with Mary Magdalene,
and Mary, the mother of Jesus,
and they lowered his body
from the cross.
They carried the body,
laid it in a tomb,
and rolled a huge stone
in front of the opening.

The next evening,
when the Sabbath was ended,
Mary Magdalene, Salome,
and Mary, the mother of Jesus,
bought embalming spices.
Early the following morning,
as the day was dawning,
Mary Magdalene and other women
went to the tomb.
When they arrived there,

they saw that the stone
had been moved aside,
and the body of Jesus
was gone.
An angel appeared
before them and said,
"Do not be afraid.
Jesus of Nazareth
is not here—
he is alive.
Didn't he tell you
that he would rise again
on the third day?"
Then, the women remembered.
They were frightened,
but full of joy.
They hurried away.
Suddenly, they looked up
and saw Jesus
standing before them.
"Don't be frightened,"
Jesus said.
"Go tell my followers
to go to Galilee,
and I will meet them there."

TOMB—is a place where the bodies of the dead are buried. The tombs in Palestine were often carved out of the rocky hillsides, like caves, and had large stones rolled against the doorways to protect the graves from robbers.

MARY MAGDALENE—(or Mary of Magdala), was described as one of the women of Galilee who gave financial help and service to Jesus and his disciples. She was present at the crucifixion and burial of Jesus, and the Gospel of John gives her the honor of being the first person to see Jesus after his resurrection. In Luke it is told that Jesus cast "seven demons" from her which is considered, today, by some to mean that she was probably an epileptic, and that Jesus cured her. Some identify her as a woman who had led an immoral life before she met Jesus, but it is not certain.

It was not easy
for his followers
to believe that
Jesus was really alive,
but, as they were told,
they traveled to Galilee.

And when they saw Jesus,
he scolded them
for doubting those
who had seen him.

After Jesus had been
with them for some time,
he told them,
"As I came from God,
I must now return.
Although I must leave you,

don't be afraid,
for you will not be alone.
My spirit
and my truth
will stay with you.
Now, you are to go
and teach all nations
and all people
what I have taught you.
Baptize those who believe,
and tell them
to live in the way
I have shown you.
Go do these things,
and I will be with you always,
even to the end of this world."

Amen.

AMEN—is a word often said at the end of a prayer or a wish. It means, so be it; may it become true.